I0108081

The Gospel
of Household Plants

The Gospel of Household Plants

poems

Brenna Lemieux

QUERCUS REVIEW PRESS
MODESTO, CA
2015

QUERCUS REVIEW PRESS POETRY SERIES
Sam Pierstorff, *Editor*

QUERCUS
Review
P   R   E   S   S

Published by Quercus Review Press
Department of English
Modesto Junior College
quercusreviewpress.com

All poems copyright © 2015 by Brenna Lemieux
All rights reserved
First Printing
Printed in the United States of America

Cover & author photo by Kristin Tirocchi
Final Judge: Stella Beratlis

Printed on acid-free paper
10 9 8 7 6 5 4 3 2 1

Except for the quotation of short passages for the purposes of criticism and review, no part of this book may be reproduced in any form or by any means without written permission of the publisher.

Requests for permissions to make copies of any part of this work should be mailed to: Permissions, Quercus Review Press, Modesto Jr. College, 435 College Avenue, Modesto, CA 95350

ISBN-13: 978-0692529102
ISBN-10: 0692529101

Publications by Quercus Review Press (QRP) are made possible with the support of the English Department at Modesto-Junior College. A portion of the proceeds from the sale of this book will benefit creative writing scholarships at Modesto Junior College.

CONTENTS

For my parents, Cindy and Albert

I.

ALL THE UNBLESSED PLANTS

Precision

When I change lanes on I-70 North
toward the St. Louis airport, my father points
to my sideview mirrors and asks
how I like them angled. He tells me
he keeps his tilted to show only a trace
of his car, a shadow, enough to see
where it ends and the asphalt picks up.
While he speaks, he leans his right palm
to show what he means, lines with his
left forefinger the wrist-hand seam
where his car peeks in.

                This type of precision
steers his whole life: gardens charted
to the inch, plates wiped clean with the heel
slice of bread, tee-shirts tucked into careful
squares
        (*But I just folded those*, I say,
and he says they'll wrinkle in the drawer
like that); his paper napkins lie neat
after meals, evenly smeared with grease.

And when he hurries (at the airport,
say, late because his daughter got lost
watching his hands instead of street signs),
he wastes no motion: veers from the car,
seizes his suitcase, and skates through the crowd
as if weightless, as if his efficiency
could humble even gravity, could tempt
even time to turn around and look.

Older Sister
—for Danielle

Though Danielle had plenty for me to covet—
dark hair, the gift of fleet reading, a sweet
singing voice—what I envied most
was her third nipple. During baths, I'd check
my trunk for a mark equally rare and splendid—
a second bellybutton, perhaps—
but all I had were allergies (to pollen,
to dander, *to all things bright and beautiful,*
she hissed across the hymnal at me the week
we'd had to give away our first and only dog).

I lacked her flair, some innate alchemy,
some DNA strand that glamorized flaws—
chickenpox blisters flecked her cheeks
like doll-freckles; her skinned knees mellowed
into scabs like peonies. She seemed more vivid,
more keenly limned than I was.
She measured rooms in cartwheels,
tap-danced during phone calls, and always asked
to stay up later; she made friends in elevators,
checkout lines, waiting rooms; she knew
what to say to old people and wasn't
afraid of the dark. Had she been a bird,
I would have dragged myself to the roof
and eaten ants; had she been a fruit tree,
I would have sunk into the soil beside her.

Each time we left the house, I'd brace myself
against the noise and clutter while she swept
through it like a pear-bloom tornado,
her skinny elegance burnished, surging,

unchecked. I'd watch her, breathless,
knowing already I would never learn
to rhyme myself with the world that way,
that I would always come as a disappointment
to people who met her first.

Ear Training

Mrs. Barlow had a heaving bosom—that's the nicest way
to say it—and during my ear training in her bright, no-muss
basement studio, when the clicking noise began above us
and my eyes roved to the ceiling, she'd say, *Don't mind him*,
and branch her fingers across the keys.

                                   I thought she meant
her husband. I pictured him hunkered upstairs,
snipping his toenails—a huge, bearded man with carapace nails
impervious to even pliers-sized clippers, impossible to trim
in less than an hour—and when I misheard an interval,
she would scold me to listen for the gap be*tween* the notes,
then the way they yoked. I strained until my ears felt
inside out, but all I heard was clicking, the threat of meeting
this grum, horn-toed man on my way out. I was a shy,
spindly child; worry came naturally.

                                   I don't know when
I realized they had a dog and linoleum floors. It occurred to me
piecemeal, around the time I came to be ashamed
of pretty much everything: my acne, my body, which tended
hopelessly toward the linear, and, above all, my inexcusably boring
localness—I would have given anything to be from elsewhere,
to celebrate strange holidays, to unpack figs and grape-leaves
at lunch, to camber my vowels into things so precisely deviant
that everyone who heard them would be charmed.

I Sit in Mrs. Eder's Sunday School Class

Never mind that her fingers are so lithe
they bow backwards, that the bones of her hands
spoke like umbrella ribs, that the bible's onion-skin
pages arch at her touch—James gazes at the crumbling
piano and Jeremy glues his eyes to the hall door,
tensed to shout when the tray of animal crackers
and juice arrives. Never mind that these passages line
her soul—*I shall not want* and *yea, though I walk*—
nor that she teared up yesterday planning this lesson,
remembering the first time she'd read the twenty-third Psalm
and understood it, just after she'd lost her second
and the doctor began to speak of *alternatives*, that she'd
so looked forward to guiding her class through it.
Kim asks to use the bathroom, Hanna wants the window
open, and when Jeremy springs to the door and thumps
the food and pitcher on the table, what can she do
but let us eat? Grace, of course, after grace.

Earl Grey

The first time I saw a man drink coffee,
he might as well have been in drag. In our house,
coffee hinted lipstick, tampons, high heels—
a woman's drink, cheap and plentiful—

my mother could brew too much and dump
the surplus guilt-free. My father drank Earl Grey.
When a cup had steeped, he'd thumb the bag
between its tag and the mug to wring

every teadrop from the leaves—drinks and habits
as gender-specific as bathing suits. Even
Laura Ingalls Wilder confirmed it—her pa dubbed
his open-prairie campfire tea a *man's drink*,

and so, when we stayed at the beach with neighbors
one summer and the father poured himself coffee
at breakfast, I was stunned—he didn't *look*
like a pervert. I watched him closely all week—

hoisting his son over waves, teaching the girls
to sculpt sand, rubbing sunblock on his wife's
shoulders. My shock faded. He seemed
perfectly normal.
                          I felt the way sunbathers

must feel when dermatologists break the news
about skin cancer, as if my eyelids had been
yanked up like roller blinds. For six days, my sisters
and I sowed drip castles by the waterline.

I wondered how the sun might feel flush
against my chest, whether it meant anything
that I didn't care for shoe shopping, if, perhaps,
even I could grow up to prefer Earl Grey.

Thumb-Sucking
—for Kristin

When the girl sucks her thumb, she tells
herself a tale: King Pointer (red-caped,
sceptered) reigns from his nose throne.
The Middle Finger queen reclines along
the upper lip—not a throne, but regal—
and the villagers, Ring Finger and Pinkie,
till the fields of her lips. When the fingers
fidget, that is obeisance, though the girl
doesn't know this word, only has a notion
from fairy tales that one must honor
a king. The thumb, then, is the dragon,
clamped in the wet dungeon so he can't
ignite the palace.
                              And that's the whole story:
king and queen above, peasants below,
the dragon packed out of sight.
Comfort in the constancy, the way her
father takes the same chair at dinner every
night, the way her mother smells tangy-
yellow when she's dressing for a party.
People say the girl will ruin her teeth.
                              People say,
You should paint those nails with turpentine.
Her mother smiles and tucks her in. She
says, *Goodnight, angel,* and kisses her cheek.
She says the girl will outgrow it and the girl
remembers outgrowing last year's church shoes
and imagines her thumb so swollen her mouth
pinches its edges and her mother slides it off
to pack in the grocery bag marked "giveaway."

My Father's Moonlilies

At twilight they unfurl for his return from work,
more patient than his daughters ever were. He shoots
whole rolls of their trumpety blossoms, tucks the images
in albums, stores their seeds in empty film canisters
and presses these on neighbors, whose plants
hardly rupture their lawns—nothing like my father's,
which sprawl and flaunt their bone-white petals.

August. He disappears after dinner and we don't see
him for hours.
　　　　　　Barefoot, I wander the yard and find
him cross-legged in his garden, head level with the smallest
moonlily, a book fanned in his lap. The flower bell turned
toward his voice. Its lifting and falling. The whisk of turned pages.

Hard to explain this: not jealousy exactly, not sadness.
A feeling like missing the bottom stair, the anticipation
of a headlong fall. Then his voice. The way each character
gets a different cadence.
　　　　　　　　　The flowers exhale a scent
like clean cotton stored in wooden drawers, old shirts
ready to be worn as smocks. I turn and tiptoe toward
the house, my feet all but bouncing off the spongy ground.

The Sun Elves

They always drove too fast,
said my mother, and the sun, stashed
in the back of their chariot,
would quake like teawater and crown
long before its time. It was their fault
our yawns could barely clear our lips
while we dressed for school in the late
winter dawn.
                    I pictured them knurl-kneed,
thread-limbed, tall and clad in bowler hats.
Rings on their spider-leg fingers,
vain and privileged with laughs
that fractured like ice.
                    So what
if it was a frivolous version
of the cosmos? We needed the elves.
We needed their chariot—
something to believe we had
a chance of grabbing and slowing
before it hurtled past us,
smelling blank as flour.

The Gospel of Household Plants

On St. Francis Day, the other parish children led their pets
to the altar to be blessed, but my allergies meant

our family owned only fish, which my sisters said
did not count, so we brought instead potted plants

and the priest, raising her eyebrows, asked for their names.
Violet, I said, lifting mine to her sign-of-the-cross hand

and she asked if I knew it was an aster. I didn't.
It had no buds, and I'd only just named it

in the car, tricked by the purple flower painted on its pot.
She conjured a blessing—*thrive from the roots* and *name of the Son*.

But at home it wilted, which struck me as rude
if not downright sinister: all my father's unblessed plants jungled

with unnerving force. Their vines writhed up the sofa back,
their sharp spines skived our legs. Abandoned in the house

too long, they'd greet us in a drunken mob of green, pollen
all but dripping from their leaves, their shadows scaling the walls

like smoke, reminding us they didn't need communion
to feast on the light of the world.

How Wars Start

Girls, enough, my mother warned us, her knuckles white-capped
on the steering wheel, weary of our constant bicker over window seats
and dress-up clothes and whose turn it was to clear the table—
                                        That's how wars start.
Whether she thought it would work, I don't know, but my sisters and I
snapped into silence. And maybe because I was just old enough
to catch snatches of the news, to read some of the headline words
on abandoned papers—

                                        something about *Oil*
                                        something about *God*—
and maybe because I inherited the family habit of worry, I believed
the war we saw that summer on TV was somehow my fault,
that I could have stopped it had I been kinder to my sisters, more patient
waiting a turn to jump rope, less surly about scrubbing silverware.

And why wouldn't I believe? I accepted that Oreos would rot my teeth,
that carrots would give me super-vision, that lit lights hurt the planet,
that when you had saved ten dollars, you could buy a troll doll
and fix its hair however you liked—I knew something about ownership,
                                        (she's in my seat,
                            she's over the line again,
                        she won't stop copying me),
about possession—
                        She looks up to you, my mother said, and,
Imitation is the highest form of flattery—
                        nothing drove me crazier than when I wanted to sing
                to myself and my older sister chimed in, just because she knew
                I hated it, hated to share the chorus, hated the invasion
                of my auditory territory, which was barren, anyway—I can't sing
                for shit—and I'd fold my arms and huff and stop altogether,
                to *show her,* which of course never worked—
I knew about the melted-glass anger that can scald you from inside
your throat, about the way a person can claw into your pores

so that to free yourself, you have to shout and flail,
you have to seethe your blood so she can't stand its heat—

$\qquad\qquad\qquad\qquad\qquad$ melt her off,

$\qquad\qquad\qquad\qquad\qquad$ smoke her out,

to *move* somehow, a scream and flung plate will do, but the best

$\qquad\qquad\qquad\qquad\qquad\qquad$ is to hit her—

one slap, neat and sharp across her face,
so that a palm print gathers like red fog,
her mouth an ax notch of surprise, her eyes
brimmed with tears from the sting—and there's one eighth-note
$\qquad$ where everything
in your whole body aligns. Harmony. Peace—or something that would
$\qquad$ be peace
if it could stay

$\qquad\qquad\qquad\qquad\qquad$ but it evaporates
and leaves behind an unwashed stone in the gut. Guilt, we call it,
$\qquad$ or Shame.
Regret,
$\qquad\qquad$ (not real regret, the I'm-going-to-pay-for-this kind),
and then fear because hitting your sister can only end a few ways,
the best of which is that she hits you back,

$\qquad\qquad\qquad\qquad\qquad$ harder.

$\qquad\qquad\qquad$ After dinner, my father would switch on
the news to scenes of smoke-bright blasts, soldiers marching
in full combat gear, anchormen in dark suits and frowns—
senseless, he'd say, shaking his head.

$\qquad\qquad\qquad\qquad$ But they never showed
the bodies. All that war footage and no corpses, no ravaged battlefields
strewn with the fallen—

$\qquad\qquad\qquad$ out of cowardice, it seems now,
some too-true fear of what the faces of the living would show
were they caught in that instant post trigger-pull, when they knew
their missile had struck home, when they felt that orgasmic purge
of their prefab hate, a rich, round glow swelling in them, better than

23

a hot shower or buttered biscuits on the tongue,
better than honey daubed on a paper-cut or the first time
you tug on new socks, better than a church choir's
perfect thirds, a maple at the peak of its gaudy
orange, the balm from a clean baby's scalp,
better than salt and gloves and coastal air scrubbing
uncovered skin—
          a pleasure we all pretend we couldn't feel,
or wouldn't feel, or won't. A pleasure easy to deny so long
as it's tucked away from the news, kept free from the bindings
of History, so long as it can waft away from all but the unlucky men
who feel it—for them, it will curdle into night sweats and road rage,
Shell Shock and Battle Fatigue and Post-Traumatic Stress Disorder.

          War is hell, we say, and it's true, because Hell
is a place where one quick beckon can land you an eternity of suffering,
of tasting razors, of noise and heat and pain pickaxing you—
if that beckon was with your trigger finger and your aim was halfway true.
War is hitting your sister over and over because you've been told to,
so often there's nothing in it but misery for you both—
          you don't hate her anymore
and then you do, for bruising, for crying, for feeling so much pain
          which means you must feel pain
          because you love her
          even when you hate her
          but you can't stop
          because that's war,
that's what it means to take orders, to follow a cause larger
than yourself or any self, to march forward boldly and tell yourself
you're grateful that someone else, at least, has decided whom
you're meant to kill, and how, has told you when and where
to march, and in what formation, and has furnished you
with high-quality, durable, all-weather boots.

II.

ARBOR
DEMENTIA

Accident

A pickle jar in my hand today splintered
at its collision with faucet water. Something
of a wind chime in its shattering—
percussive-melodic tinkling, glass leaping
away from itself in long-e whistles. A shard
lodged in the bend of my wrist, the part
where veins converge and freckles don't, violet
through meringue, palm-forearm estuary—
but not so much blood—a salmon bloom
that stilled once I rolled clear the hole
and sucked, combing my other hand
through the dishwater for drowned fragments.

Most of the larger pieces still hinted at the jar—
torso arc and knee-bend—and I thought
of my mother, who called to tell me a Southern
Leopard Frog was found in the Chesapeake Bay
this week with two extra legs. Even as my flesh
knits itself together, an environmental biologist
somewhere vivisects this frog, faints from the cloud
of fermented nitrogen that bursts from it. Collapses
eye-first into her own scalpel, head-cracks
the table and slides to the floor. A heap
of lab coat and loose hair. And on the table,
blood oozing, forelegs twitching, the frog blinks.

The Tree Suicides

And those that didn't kill themselves went mad,
bloomed in mid-winter and dumped their leaves
weeks later, spouted sap from knotholes, arched
their roots so that trail reports of tripping injuries
soared; one white oak known for its branch-span
took to hurling acorns, causing more than one
concussion.
                                        Edwin Marsh,
the country's lone tree psychologist, tried to drum
up civic concern, but even the public radio folks
brushed him off, suspecting a hoax. The suicide
rate mounted—no root girdling, no apparent trunk
trauma, just a full halt to photosynthesis and
nutrient absorption. Analysts whipped out *climate
change* and *El Niño* like corporate credit cards—this'll
take care of it, the sentiment ran, it's not our mess.

Edwin loathed the thought of reframing the crisis,
but instead of knotting themselves in protest chains,
people surfed the web, hit snooze, requested extra
espresso shots. So how else to convince
them of the problem's scope except point out
that dry wood eventually sparks and blazes
and spews enough smoke to clog everyone's lungs,
that it leaves any survivors to breathe nothing
but unbroken, ash-thick wind? How else, indeed,
he thought, tossing the first struck match.

Dream

Through the storm's rubble, I drag feet-first
the cedar statue my mother has become—
crudely hewn, unvarnished, lips and hair a rough
umber. Her heels chafe and splinter my palms.

Among the soaked boards and leveled
conifers, a man in boots bends and straightens,
picking his way through the wreckage to anoint
the fallen with paint. He bows and daubs
a statue's mouth. It gasps and shakes
into flesh, tremors rippling its limbs. I offer
my mother and he paints her hair first,
then her lips. Laughing, she pinches my forehead.
You have dust mites in your skin, she says, and plucks
a squirming bug, squashes it with her nails. I know
she means *termites,* that I've caught them
tending her. I find a mirror and see my cheeks
wriggle with shadows, so I dig and squeeze
the insects one by one, until my face resembles
the ruins around me. *Hurricane,* I repeat
to myself, and wake up craving milk.

Migration

Hundreds of grackles squawk from the web
of branches, their chirm like sidewalk vendors
hawking gaudy wares. All at once, they hush,
as if tamped by the oyster-shell clouds, then rush
up, thrash the air and shoot southward
with the sweeping sureness I first heard
in my mother's voice some February night when fat,
wet snowflakes slapped the windshield and melted
and she sighed, *They'll never close school for this*,
and made everyone pack lunches before bed.

A certainty thick with regret, like that of stage
hands striking a set, or of the ancients who claimed
the earth grew like an acorn, its sky star-pocked,
accessible, a heel's grind removed from dust.

Elegy for the G in Onion

My whole life, I've been saying *onion* wrong,
the way my father does, with a *g* tacked
on the first half, *ongion*, which I've only just grasped
is a relic of his dinnertable French, his parents'
language, stubborn as an onion's bite on the tongue.
Now I say it right and the word feels meager,
unanchored, and last weekend I craved that *g* so badly
I found myself in the grocery store murmuring
strangulate, granular, ignoble, globe.

The *g* is what lingers, what snags when we speak.
If *g* is the gate between generations, I'm swinging
on its hinge away from my grandfather's overgrown
horseshoe pits, from his widow's unflagging gestures,
those bits of oral punctuation that help her salvage
half-translated words from the ether.

I get my *g*s from granola, egg whites, gluten-free bagels—
nothing like the tangy garden *g* in *oignon*, the gruff
waste *g*s in *gaspillage*, the almost-noble *grenouille*,
which means frog, an animal that gurgles ceaseless
*g*s free from the cumbrance of words.

But I only know this because I studied
French in school. I was born assimilated,
raised to brag of baguette-and-ongion roots
because they don't crimp my speech—I boast
of preferring white bread, as if it verifies
my heritage.
                    What I mean is that in this country,
foreignness begets shame until the third
generation, when sameness has planed us

so flat we're desperate for gnarls—we'll latch
onto anything that might draw a stranger's gaze,
even a vegetable that stings our eyes,
even the ghost of a leftover letter
fogging like bad breath from our gums.

Someone Else's Pain

—for J.B.

You, who exult in fatigue, whom sweat salves,
whom motion girds like prayer, try to tell me
calmly that your new meniscus (transplanted
last summer, not yet healed) has torn, or turned,
or that scar tissue has crept between your ligaments—
you're not sure—some driven-screw anguish
that flares when you move, gluts your knee
with heat;
                your voice climbs in coils that you catch
and unsnarl before they snap, as if tuning a loose-
dialed radio, twisting out each snore of static,
and all I can do is nod or shake my head, offer
the sturdy focus I once used in art class to smudge
graphite across a page, trying in vain to capture
the way shadows defined my unclasped hand.

You Visit the Deserted Asylum

At a bend in the road, the building crests
before you like a lion braced on its forelegs.
He enters and you follow—the smell of gym class
and rot. Birds plunging from the dark. In every
room, *devices*: clamp-fitted metal chairs, straps
riveted to walls, gurneys on wheels. Graffiti,
trash, a tree stabbed through an upstairs window.
I'm waiting outside, you say and he shakes his head.

You're quiet on the way back and walk faster,
baffled to find that you do not want to hold
his hand, that you balk when he catches your elbow
to steer you from a puddle. The thing is, his sunscreen
has worn off. Without it, he smells ordinary.

The Signal

The roadside crows swarm the cornstalks
and church-spire upward, thick and black
as blown cinders—I can't look away.
I'm going forty on the highway
and I'll probably miss my plane.

Things weren't always this way—I lived
near my family and drove fast. The edges
of the world stayed pinned down.

But now sunlight unravels my eyes in watery
threads; I see the horizon peeling, hear rust
gnawing my car. Soon, I know, the road
will crumble and buck me and I'll land chin-first,
come to with gravel on my tongue, crows plucking
my scalp for nests.
                    Soon, I know, but not when.
With crows, anything could be the signal.

After the Derecho

I'd never seen anything like it,
winds straight and fast
                    as a freefall,
my umbrella ribs cracked, ripped
through the nylon, thunder
that shoulder-slammed my front door—
afterward, Carbondale hung
in tatters, trees sprawled across streets
and sidewalks, their mud-tamped roots
jutting like capsized dinner tables.

Walking anywhere meant dodging
downed power lines
and windshield shards, wrestling
grit-thick branches—for weeks,
my hands never quite felt clean.
My landlord ignored my calls
about the tree on the roof—

when the wind rose, its branches beat
my front window, as if begging
for deliverance from the torment
of woodlice—I could see them gnawing
through its trunk into the house's
wooden frame.

                    I pushed my furniture
in from the walls, bumped into it so much
my skin purpled and took on the mashed
texture of rotten bark. My last nights there,
I lay in bed rigid, too tender to turn
or flick away the lice, whose hunger

I could almost hear raging inside them
like a fire tearing outward
from the last of a smoking woods.

Arbor Dementia

Walking home, I squint through streetlight at ash
branches arched like my grandmother's cursive,
filmy with new blooms—winter clenched the city
so long the spring-frilled streets seem foreign.

For a moment, I'm lost. A blunt rasp drones
in my ear. My entire body itches—
                                        I wonder whether
my mind is leaching away as my grandmother's did,
so that we whispered *dementia* and pocketed the keys
to her Oldsmobile. That fall, when my sister and I
drove it to school, she found a bottle of dish soap
stuffed beneath the seats, squeezed a palmful
and splayed her fingers out the window, certain
that a clutch of bubbles would erupt and scroll
behind us as we drove.
                                        Now, walking home,
I see traces of the Emerald Ash Borers.
Their victims shoot new sprouts and die, bark carved
with the borers' gaudy print. I scratch behind my ear
and find one, gleaming green, which explains
why everything I hear sounds chafed, why my skin
feels sheathed with holes, why the man I love
just sent me home for good and I've walked
the whole way trying to read the nonsense-script
of ash trees, trying to hear anything
in the clotting purple citydusk,
its battery of hungry consonants.

A Father's Prejudice

He mistrusts wind, how it whittles
every room it enters. At six, his daughter

pitched down concrete steps and struck
an iron railing, blood and rust spattering

her face. He cradled her to his shirt
and shook his head—water

would have caught her. But then, water
can be tricky too: when she was born,

he watched doctors try and try to drain
her breathless lungs while lupine blue

gathered like dusk in her skin
and a nurse glanced up at the clock.

Portrait of the Artist in a Dugout Canoe

Suppose I felled a Douglas fir, scraped it hollow,
scooped its center out, fashioned paddles
from its boughs, waded into a lake, pushed off
and began to row. A lake big enough to get lost on,
somewhere north of here, and east.

If you accept the premise, the rest follows: blisters
hump along my palms, the insides of my thumbs,
my finger-crooks—now and then a splinter pierces—
heat swells my veins, heat that is the ache of one stroke
perpetually hooped, the plunk and score of paddles
culling water, the graph paper horizon of x
approaching infinity, and x is nothing, a variable,
the silence at the end of my name. This isn't about x,
it's about my spine flattened along the bottom
of a dugout canoe, my feet pressed to its wooden hull,
the lake's throb beneath me, the air's bite
of rotting leaves and pines whip-stitched with dew.

The boat skims the lake's center and I've passed
into a filmy sleep that laps at me as water laps the canoe.
Long before dawn, I startle awake.
Bunched clouds plunge from the sky and ripen
into a rain-woman whose rain hair ripples, flecked
with light—she dives to my vessel, perches
on its edge, and chides me in a language
that sounds like an owl weeping, all open vowels
and moisture. Behind her, the moon pulses,
lights her face, and I see
                              she's me, as I will look
when I die and cede my body to weather patterns
(a surrender like falling asleep, when the body

rolls in on itself like a pair of socks).

The clouds collect again and churn the sky, cast
their pewter image on the lake. From the woods,
a wren warbles and rouses others, whose squawks rise
to a sour din: morning has burst somewhere. The woman
reaches her watery hand to my face, a palm
like fish scales and chilled wine. Her form dissolves
and splashes into the canoe, where she sloshes
around me and rocks, tips the vessel, and the sky ruptures
and rain pelts the lake and me, and by the time
I realize what's happened, I'm already half drowned.

III.

THIS IS HOW
THE FIRE
BEGAN

We Were Waiting

The trees undress as gradually as parents
after a dinner party and everything outside
smells smoky. Burnt-wick branches,

leaves drifted like spent flames—as if hundreds
of front lawns flared and snuffed to brace
themselves for winter. One night, a mother

and father return whispering, slip off
their shoes and tiptoe to kiss their daughters'
foreheads. Her earrings unclasp in her fingers,

a glass fills with tapwater at his touch.
Upstairs, he tugs her zipper—her dress curls
from her shoulders and sifts to the floor.

Their bare limbs sway into each other.
In family legend, this is how the fire began:
castoff party clothes like leaves, arms and legs

like twigs, the house itself a furnace. The parents
woke to find their hair singed gray, their skin
dry and wrinkled, their daughters' beds empty,

ash collected on the pillows. *It happened so quickly,*
said the father. *Yes,* said the mother,
And we didn't even realize we were waiting for it.

Ballroom Dancing Class

Cindy has a pentagram face and a body
like a lilac leaf—all curves below
and angles on top. Soft-shoed, her steps
so fluid you forget she has legs,
she glides like wax down a candle, the scent
of coffee and pinecones in her wake.

The instructor, Ron, who's in love with her,
calls her to demonstrate each new step:
Notice how my fingers barely brush the lady's arm,
he drawls, trawling her across the gym.
She winks past him at her husband,
who rolls his eyes.
                    But he understands—
he remembers when they first met,
when he couldn't sleep for mulling the slope
of her shoulders or the rise of her calves,
when he'd raid the grocer's spice and produce aisles
to replicate her scent (cloves, bay leaves,
unripe pears), aching to his liver with insomnia,
dizzy as a gauze curtain in a storm.

Departures

I sledded into a tree once, saw
what would happen halfway down the hill
but couldn't slow or steer, just felt
my bones shrink with a helpless,
thrilling terror, which is exactly
what meeting John felt like.

- *July* -

I'd knead my neck at work and picture
Montana, John stitching blisters
on his feet, the needle sterilized with matches
because alcohol weighs down a rucksack.
He packed light but still he burst a disc,
its gel lapped onto a nerve, which feels,
he says, like someone holding a flame
to the bones, like tingling and numbness,
or like hell, depending on his mood.

When he left, he discarded a last box
of belongings, the contents sagged
with their own weight. He wanted nothing
to *belong* to him; he wanted to be long
in the mountains, alone with his castoff Army
bag, first issued to K. Benecke, whom I guessed
was Kevin and he said probably Ken.
Its pristine condition had hinted grief more
than fastidiousness, irrelevant and potent grief,
which I had no strength for and ignored.

I offered to take his stuff to Good Will,
and so returned to my apartment box-laden

while John marched south to the bus. At home
I drank coffee till my eyelids purred and scrawled
on the calendar: *July, a month for departures.*

- August -

John hefts crates of cabbages and tugs up beets.
I level mountains of papers with a red pen.
The harvest in, he drifts to California, finds work
at a megachurch, and lies on his faith pledge.

I execute eighteen mice for shitting in the kitchen.
He sighs in the way of snow-cumbered trees,
so that he's lighter after and an avalanche begins
(his own, eastward) and settles on the dotted line

of our lease. We root out an old laundry set,
some secondhand pans, sit on the porch sticky nights
and slap cards on the table. Sometimes, I roll pasta,
hours of sifting and pinching, the noodles briny

from my sweat. Sometimes, I call him from the shower
and draw back the curtain. Little thrills.
We travel together and he never packs the Army bag—
I haven't seen it since the move. I'd like to ask

where he put it, what he thinks happened
to its first owner. I'm ready now, I could ponder that,
as long as my hands were busy in the kitchen:

>He enlisted right after high school
>(flour talcs my arms), acned,
>the age of my students, who aren't
>so much younger than I am,

patriotic (my shoulders burn
with kneading), at least at first—
but then he comes home and marries
his highschool sweetheart
and it's summer and there's no
hint of breathable air—

(The mattress needs to be in the kitchen, he sees, with the window unit—
it's the only room that ever gets cool. He hasn't slept in weeks. Who puts
a window unit in a fucking kitchen anyway? Ninety-four degrees inside
and humid. No circulation. Bedroom feels like a goddamn sauna. He
shakes his wife, says he's taking the mattress, but she doesn't wake up,
just shifts her weight and he shouts that he's moving the goddamn mat-
tress and she can either help or see where gravity dumps her, and that
gets her, the shouting, and she sort of scissor-kicks her legs and her feet
smack the floor and he's already lifting the head corner and she lurches
to the foot and grabs it and starts talking real low, the way she has since
he got home, saying okay now, easy does it. Her slim arms go ropey,
straining against the load, and he remembers he likes that, the way her
hair's all messy too, and pauses a second to watch her but she keeps go-
ing and sort of butts into the mattress. In the kitchen, he slides it across
the tile and it flops flat, blowing a draft, and he sees right away this will
work, he'll be able to sleep here, and strides to the bedroom for a pillow
and when he returns she has a glass of ice water and she's saying why
don't you drink this, saying I'm worried you're dehydrated and it looks
delicious and he gulps it and feels better even though it kind of sloshes
in his stomach after. He lies down and she refills the glass and sets it by
his head and switches off the light and he doesn't notice falling asleep
but suddenly he's back in Iraq and everything's exploding around him
and inside him and all he can think is I shouldn't have had that water
because it's oozing out his stomach and everyone thinks that it's blood
and he's dead and he tries to shout but can't and can't move and they zip
him up and now he really might die because there's no air and he wakes
tensed, sweat-greased, his wife kneeling beside him breathing *sh* and

swabbing his forehead, which feels ready to split like a
tree-root sidewalk.)

                         —never mind. I don't want to do this.

But it's no good. The soldier's loose now,
it's his poem too.
                    Fine then.
                                        K. Benecke,
you shipped to Iraq and it scorched you.

You leaked into my life and I ignored you.
I hang a peace sign flag in the living room,
as if it absolves me.

                    Mr. Benecke—

This was meant to be a love poem.

On Elm Street

Metallic porch-screen dust at my nose jolts me
awake—sleepwalking again.
                                        Outside, leaves writhe,
undersides fleshy and pale. Lightning throbs
like the vein in a boxer's forehead and oaks buck,
exposing themselves to the wind, shuddering
at each charged ruck. Rain pummels our lawn to liquid.

The floor creaks and John pads to me, flattens his palm
on my shoulder blades. His night smell mixes
with the petrichor—rain, earth, cotton, salt—
So much for the drought, he says, yawning. I lean into
him and think of bananas curved against each other,
ripening in synch. *It's all right*, I say, *we can get the dryer fixed.*
He rests his chin on my head and lightning flares, reveals
the neighbor's trashcans thudding down the street.

March in Galway

Without warning, the pedestrian clump
I'm struggling against forks; its prongs spread
and crimp around a plodding couple—
I pass on their right, light and giddy as smoke
twining from a cigar, blood thrumming
like a cymbal roll in my ears—for this instant,
I am one human-sized cell in the living
organism of Shop Street—I dodge a lamppost
as if each step were plotted, rehearsed:
here a child will toddle through the crowd,
here a man will slow to check his phone—
I skirt them all, deft as a threadfin
flitting in its school—then clip the corner
and land in another bog. Whatever spell
harmonized us has faded. Our steps pound
out of synch, our voices clash: collisions
at the pub doors, the double-fast clack
of hurried businesspeople, sandwich papers
crinkling as the rushed finish lunch and swipe
sleeves across their mouths. Even the living
statue has gone restless—ahead of me, his
pewter-painted back disappears toward the river,
a host of gawking, blue-clad schoolboys in his wake.

Two Purple Sponges
—Galway, Ireland

The street magician whisks gloved fingers
down the boy's cream-smooth arm then taps
his fist. When the boy unclenches, two purple sponges
bloom in his palm.
                           He gasps. In the grace-note
of their growth, he's consumed, has no idea
when they'll stop, and, like an urge to hit his sister,
a hope flits through him that they'll go on
swelling forever, or until they're so large his arms
can't span them, like his cousins' beanbag chairs,
only lighter, springier, better for falling into
because they'd hurtle him back—but in a flash,
they're finished, the size of ripe crabapples.
His mother drops a fiver in the box,
so the magician bows and waves her off.

At home, the boy wrings and releases them himself
to see how far they'll spread (perhaps a little further
at each squeeze, he thinks, so little he won't notice
at first), then slips them in a jar and calipers them
each morning with a slack pinch. They never grow,
of course, but his whole life he has an inkling
that the sponges are somehow charmed, and feels silly
when he moves out years later and packs them.
They're chunks of dusty foam, he knows, but has never
really seen them that way, will never see them, perhaps,
without a white-glove frame, without the thrill
of an afternoon alone with his mother, without the kind
of hope that lets a child think a sponge might be magical,
the same way he thinks that one night his da' might return
from the races, eyes unblurred, wallet bulging.

On Bridge Street

I pass a girl laughing gape-mouthed, her teeth
gapped and jagged as glass in cement walls;
seeing me, she clamps her lips. I shouldn't stare;
I'm shocked not that her mouth looks like a prison
barrier, but by the way it snaps, like a mousetrap
(*thwack* and it's over; the fine steel frame has cracked
the lattice of bones, and the corpse feels,
as it's gathered, warm and slight as a child's
gloved hand).
        Her eyes dim and she hitches
the groceries higher on her chest with the air
of someone raising a drawbridge for the night.

The Living Statue Speaks

It's not a matter of prolonged stillness;
you have to stop thinking in minutes and hours—
those are only on clocks. You have to
become bronze. When you do, time crumbles
like rust: when I work, I *am* ninety
percent copper and ten percent tin. Neither
of those itches, neither gets hungry or has to sneeze,
neither cares when pigeons shit on its sleeve.
People see me when I'm not working,
ropey arms, ropey legs, and they ask if I run,
ask how many miles I do. I don't run, I tell them,
I eat time. Snap that fucker's neck and get
my jaws around it like a snake. And
even then I'm not killing it—can't even get
its attention. That's the problem—
we act like time is neutral. Time's the same thing
as Death and it backhands all of us and that's that.
At least I've got my dukes up, at least
I can make a living off it, leave a couple
dings in those acres of glittering paint.

But Instead of Making the Bed

I slide under its covers and let their weight
collect as warmth in my bones—frost flecks
the window-edge and outside the world hums along,
gray and windy-wet.
                              I know someone who loves
apples so much he closes his eyes to chew—
Jongagold, he'll say, or *Gala*, the way some people
say *Amen*, and that's how good this bed feels,
crisp-sheeted, dense, sweet with the smell
of fresh laundry and hair.
                              We need groceries.
I should be tugging on boots and gathering bags.
I should be brushing the last wrinkle from
the quilt and wrapping scarves around my neck
and checking whether the trash needs emptying
on the way out. *You about ready?* John calls
from downstairs and I say I am, one minute,
but remain supine and flex my toes and count
to forty before heaving back the covers
and letting them flop into a tangle at the foot
of the bed, untidy as a heap of grimy snow.

Umamiskin (a Love Poem)

Salt all over the counter, baby—not just grains,
either, coarse kosher tablets of sodium chloride,
parched and pebbly as a grain of beach lodged
in your molar that cracks like a dropped pot
when you bite down, scouring out every
filling you ever blew a paycheck on, scraping
enamel like a vandal in a china shop. But you know
to beware when you add sugar, gulp coffee,
rinse with vinegar, breathe tobacco, smoke water
bongs—it all stains your teeth and you'll be up
to your gums in dental debt before the year's out.

And sweetheart, how did we reach a stage
where it's not strange to praise the flavor of each other's
organs? Oh my dear, dear saltyliver, sourlung,
umamiskin, let's buy a value-pack of sponges
and resell them for a profit! Let's start collecting
terra-cotta bells! The newscaster says
a man three towns east just sang the lowest note
on record and gives all his thanks to whiskey
and sweater vests, which makes his wife beam
at the camera and raise a needle-stabbed hank of yarn.
My love, there's no telling how much popcorn
I could eat right now, so never mind the spill;
sweep that pile into the shaker and keep the oil hot.

IV.

THE PROBLEM OF FEALTY

Soliloquy with Salt & Water (for a Husband)

Little things. Last month, she made brownies
and mistook salt for sugar. We laughed,
but she did it again this week, and yesterday
she walked past me smelling farm-sour, like dung
and hard work—I can't remember when she last
mentioned laundry. And of course, the missed
electric bill.
           I'm having a new dream now:
pacing the shore of the lake, but it's churning
like a river, droplets spraying my face, mud underfoot
and I lose my balance and slide underwater
and I see her, wearing that red mackintosh
she had when we met, which means, in the dream,
that she will drown, and then she *has* drowned
and I'm groping for her but I can't open my eyes
and the water's tugging me down—

what I feel is relief. All I can do
is grit my teeth and swim. Because come morning
I'll have to shove the stuck door of her mind,
make sure she swallows her pills and doesn't leave
the house alone and turns the burners off.
I'll have to grab her wrists in time when she misses
the last step, make sure she changes clothes.
Her memory catheter, I joked last week, but her eyes
went blank, like someone else's coffee mug
you weren't supposed to wash.

Lake Winnipesaukee

In the waist-high water by the dock,
Gigi performs her liturgy of lifting and bending,
her Exercises, her thirty-minutes-a-day,
three-days-a-week bobbing and stretching
and clutching the pier—the same ritual
for twenty years.
                              Finished, she waddles
to shore for an afternoon of rock sifting
while we splash in the lake, her goal to rid
Cedar Cove of every unwanted stone—
should she catch us lobbing one, we're shooed
in to retrieve it. And did we wash our hands
before eating, she demands, and warns again
of Duck Itch, which, she says, will blotch us
scarlet and burn so much we'll wish we'd drowned.

But what fills her mind all these hours, winnowing
stones from the sand, her grandchildren's voices
glancing across the water? Memories of the war,
perhaps, of cocktail parties, the heady blitz
of nicotine, of men she dated and turned down—

or maybe she imagines my twenty-something
grandfather squinting from the shore at her,
the way he saw her then, dark in the noon glare,
her thin arms blading the surface, stroke

            by stroke
                        by stroke.

Cohabitation

You and I have just fought and now
I'm iron-rodded to the sofa, as if my blood's
gone rigid in my veins—to anyone outside
our warped front window, I would seem
ricked in on myself like a browned apple
core, though I feel ordinary, unfolded.

On the radio, an aging artist recalls planting
himself at his dying lover's bedside, inking
portrait after portrait of the man—yes, he tells
the interviewer, even the lesions, even
the packing-box jawline—he speaks
of the room's stark sounds, the scritch
of his pen's steel nib, the whir and blip of pulse
monitors—he says he strung wire along
the walls to hold the pictures while they dried.
And later—after—when the sheets
had been stripped and the windows lifted,
the paper snapped in the wind, a hundred times
the dead man, flattened, and his vacant bed.

If I could draw you, John, I would—full-page
sketches, profile portraits, scenes of you raking
the yard. I'd pin them to our clothesline
and let rain bleed the ink and mash the paper
to pulp. And when they dropped, I'd leave them
in the root-wrenched soil, to see what kind of flavor
they brought that fall to our apples.

My Grandmother's Nightmare Returns

She eases across the Steinway's bench, pads
her fingers on its keys. An audience blossoms
around her, faces raised in every seat,
but each key is unbuckled from its hammer,
each string snapped. Draped in new wires,
repairmen swarm the stage to restring while she
plods on. The steel slips and lengthens, sags
in the piano's gaping mouth. Keys clatter
like china trembling in an earthquake.
And her cigarette: she can't keep it settled
in her mouth.
                        The dream has lodged
in her core now, its panic threaded her veins.
Her tongue sprawls, laps over her molars,
unruly as a struggling mackerel; she's forgotten
how to taste sounds when they form and disperse—
a bit like blowing smoke rings, a bit like licking
stamps. Objects have un-buckled from their names—
toast is lost, and *radio*, and *egg*, as if her brain
were rattling in her skull, dropping words
like loose tobacco, and she'll no sooner recover them
than piano pedals will bloom above the keys'
gumline, than a fishhook will sprout a teacup.

Three-Fingered Willy

The legend says he was a builder: fitting a cabin
window, he lost his balance, fell from a ladder,
and saw, before fainting, the glass pane
scythe his bones. He woke patched and half-handed,

his ruined fingers already trashed.
He never got over it, kept hoping he'd find them,
combing the lakeside and the Wolfeboro shops,
taking what he could, what he felt the place owed him—

shoes, spare towels, foodscraps—though what he wanted
was fingers, and campers were warned to sleep
cross-armed and clench-clawed—
this is the story you were always told.

No wonder, then, that years later, when you're grown,
dozing on your grandparents' sofa and the floorboards
moan, you cut your breath. The wind swells; a bough
raps the window. No wonder you have to remind yourself

that Three-Fingered Willy is a myth, a joke, a rogue
cooked up to spook your grandfather's campers,
before the camp folded and its land was sold
for houses (for this house, in fact). Why, then,

this lake-water chill to the air? Why the heft
of another soul in the room?
                              You hoop your eyes
but see only woolen air, its gloom of unlit roads
and feral birch woods, the sort of stone-fisted night

that chokes New Hampshire summers, windy
and so dark every branch-snap and leaf-crunch
could be a lurker, a bandit, a vagabond alone
too long, nurturing a mean streak,

who wants more from you than your smokes
and the Tootsie Rolls you bought in town today.
The neighbor's ax went missing this week.
No one thinks it was stolen for splitting wood.

Dysphasia

She used to sleepwalk, we'd find her all over
The house and she'd wake sort of grace— grant—

Sort of grade— … bit by bit. Stamp her foot when
We laughed at her tell her drums— her dreams.

And now she snips so fast to me, her voice
Bends around itself … I can't remember how to say it.

Everyone speeches so much quicker than ago … Night
Crouches and leaps at us, see? It was just here! She

Flitters around like a humanbird— a humidbird …
And when she talks to me I can't prosper the suds.

Can't *process* the *sounds*. Too speeded. Nobody *senses*
Anymore. Nobody *makes*. But I know her, I'm *me*.

I'm *here*, Cindy! Here I am! Little bits, I can do.
Say I store a word *there*, lock away how the *Sss* hums

My teeth, the *nnn* between the lips, the *eee* like smiling,
Then the whole thing crumbles, her name an arc—

An ax— … her name a circus tumbler in my mouth.
What do I mean …? I try to hold it. And I

Practition saying it but it sponges away. *I put it right there!*
Everything melts together, so when I open to hello her,

It's gone. I taste sand. *I'm your dawn tern*, she says, which
Means the hook-pull in my stomach when she fills the

67

Doorway. Her fingers in my skill— my scald. Above. Blank
Weight and its spread, dry puddle on my legs. Picnic weather.

A field of warm stones beneath my skin.

My Grandmother's Girdle

The problem, my mother said, handing it to me, was a plastic
support strip burst from its hull, jabbing at Gigi's skin.
The problem, I saw, was my deft fingers, my sharp eyes,

my handiness with needles; it was fealty: I had sprung
from the loins that had sprung from the loins that this ancient,
liniment-rank, gray and fraying garment so futilely fought

to contain. *She didn't even wash it?* I said. Its cloth felt sticky, as if
she'd stored it too near her cough drops. It hung in a bag
from my bedroom doorknob for weeks, its odor a constant scolding.

When she asked about it I blamed homework, practice,
said *this week for sure*. She had a stroke and I draped coats
and towels over the bag, twisted it shut to dull the smell,

graduated and moved out and when I returned that February
for her funeral, it was gone.
                              Maybe my father found it,
patched it and apologized for the delay. Or else my mother did:

her dead mother's girdle, torn, greasy, unrepaired, though it needed
just a few quick stitches. And if so, she would have smelled it,
as we do with the clothes of our dead, and remembered—what?

Being seven, sleeping with a slip clutched in one fist? Talcum-dry air,
sneaking lipstick before high school? The final months,
when her mother unpegged herself from geography and time,

when she asked after folks dead for decades and began to smell
of wax and menthol even after sponge baths? Or maybe
what came to her was a scene from that last Christmas:

Gigi wearing her new hat and gloves at the table, the pale blue
fleece so pure-looking that we all flocked to her—to feel how soft,
we said, but really because we were suddenly charmed by her round nose,

her unmuscled skin, her sparse, silky hair—we rubbed her shoulders,
smoothed her head, held her hands while she giggled and squirmed,
thrilled to be touched so lavishly, to see clearly so many faces

that had been blurred for years, perpetually withdrawing from her own.

V.

BREATHING
LESSONS

Limen

A morning when my fingers smell of fermented grapes—
leaves clutter my neighbor's lawn like an army
of dead starfish, hinges creak in the rising wind,
doors crash against their frames—gradual, fierce applause
for the coming winter.

On the radio, the story of a woman whose cats kept
dying from radon in the basement—Ginger, Sam, Toby,
Ace—instead of burying them, she had them skinned
and sewn into throw pillows for the sofa. When a home
inspector told her of the leak, she begged him, wheezing,
to leave it another week or so—Elsie on the way out,
and the living room nearing a full set.

Suddenly, in my pantry, a potato so old it has burst
into blossom, reddish feelers pushing out all around its
lumpy mass, so hearty looking, so alien.
                                            I feel like I'm crouching
in the thresholds of a crumbling house: orgasm, potatobloom,
fragrant purple stain—wine, which has no memory of itself
and helps me have the same.
                                    Maybe rain will pelt
the neighborhood tonight, leave the earth muddy and ripe
for planting; maybe my hands will regenerate their webbing,
cut away at birth. Maybe somewhere, a fish is clapping for me.

My Mother Speaks of Popcorn

I met Albert one of those nights I couldn't stand
to stay home—the cats were hungry, I was hungry,
no paycheck till Friday—the Sawmill
had a popcorn maker in the corner. If you ordered
a beer and drank it slow, you could eat enough
to get full. It was that or ask my ex for money
and I'd already done that and it was—. Well.
I filed those papers for a reason.

In those days it was so *fresh* to relax in a bar,
no husband getting louder, no worry about how high
the tab was getting and whether we'd have enough
to cover it—so there I sat, munching away
and deciding what I'd order from the menu
if I had money and in walks this cute guy with a beard.

*

I didn't like cooking, but Albert said popcorn
was easy. Oil first, he said, switching on my stove,
and the test kernels. Once they pop, you add the rest.
(But how much oil, I asked, how many kernels?)
Enough oil to cover the pan, enough kernels
to soak up the oil—like cooking with Confucius.

(And what if I scorch the pot, what if I ruin
a whole batch? What if the oil starts smoking
and sets off the alarm and everyone
has to evacuate and it's all my fault?)

The kernels *smack*ed and he poured in more,
the corn tinkling like those rainsticks hippies

liked, and he showed me how to gauge it,
how to shake the pot on the burner, how to tilt it
so only the popped kernels escaped.
He didn't burn himself once.
And knowing how much salt, he said, is an art.

*

When the girls were born, the house became a cosmos
of potential death—the staircase could snap necks,
the window screens could split and drop a body—

even popcorn could wedge itself in a throat.
Albert thought to bite off the edges so no one
would choke, and Danielle would beg to stay up late

with us—we let her so long as she didn't talk
through *Cheers*—one peep and it's bedtime,
we'd say, and she'd sit there and tuck those kernels

in her mouth and I realized I had no idea how
to explain the billion complexities of her tiny body,
would never be able to heal a cut for her or expel

a virus, that her unconscious cells I'd somehow
created would do it all inside her, and suddenly
the room felt pitch-floored and stuffy.

*

Our popcorn pot broke years ago:
the lid's handle unstuck one night
halfway through a batch—no idea
how Albert managed to finish

without burning his hand. He
started fixing it the next day—
superglue with a brick on top,
some sort of clamp—the repairs
last a while and then the handle
melts off again. I bought a replacement,
but he says it's unbalanced.
Too bulky on a hot burner. The lid
doesn't vent right. He says they don't
make pots like they used to; everyone
uses the microwave these days.
So he keeps mending the old one.

*

We'll have it for dinner now sometimes,
the two of us. Easier than cooking,
and we don't need to set an example anymore.
Some Fridays when I get home, he's
already popping a batch and the oily smell
billows when I open the door.

All these years and I still can't believe
how time bolts, how popcorn always tastes good:
one second, I'm thinking something salty
would hit the spot and the next,
I'm looking at a few husks in an empty bowl,
tonguing a hull from my teeth,
grease like a glove on my hand.

Breathing Lessons

On the Baltimore side of our video chat, my father
is giddy about the salad he brought to the neighbors'
Olympics party, which, he says, he garnished
with four pepper rings and an onion slice—and here
he loops his thumbs and forefingers, overlaps
and leapfrogs them in lieu of words—*the Olympic seal*,
he explains, his hands flush with the camera.

This is nothing new: the year Aunt Ruth
had a stroke on my birthday and no one had time
to bake, he slung pancakes on the griddle, topped
them with candles and sang to me. Summers, he'd slice
cucumber donuts, flick his wrist so that broccoli
and dip became *trees in snow*. To cheer me
from a skinned knee once, he traced a ketchup *B*

on his burger (*Look*, he said, turning his plate,
B for Brenna).
                        And yet the whole time
he must have felt feverish with the need to teach us
more, to bequeath something that would last longer
than a balanced meal, to divulge a secret
like photosynthesis, that miracle he'd watched
again and again in his gardens—green things

unfolding in gasps, gulping the sun and soil
and wind—I've read that in some countries, people buy
mud as a snack. I've read you can meditate so hard
you disappear. In the Himalayas, breatharians
grow plump on air, and I wonder if my father
might be on to them, if he might be closer than any of us

has guessed to gleaning from oxygen some sign
of how it might be eaten, how to season it with sunlight,
if he might next weekend display for the camera
a legal-pad sketch of a plant cell and explain,
his fingers weaving and kneading in the roles of sun
and CO_2, how to breathe in such a way
that I can stop buying groceries forever.

Mislaid Memory about Pigeons

On the phone today, my mother asks if I remember the afternoons
my sister had choir practice, when we'd wait for her in the car

and, to pass time, give voices to the birds that preened and swooped
on the slate church roof: a battered pigeon would coast in

and I'd say, *Looks like George failed his math test,*
or two would squawk and rumple their feathers and I'd whisper,

that one didn't do his chores—
                                                        but I don't. I want
to believe it's me and not one of my sisters she's thinking of,

that I was the sort of window-gazing child who pinned her thoughts
and worries onto things that could fly. I can picture the parking lot,

the soft cotton turtlenecks I favored then, the gap
that spaced my front teeth in all my school photos,

but I have no memory of the birds. And why would I? Those afternoons,
I was knotted with longing to be the sister inside the church,

the one with the dulcet voice who stood straight and sang in the holy
            quiet,
the one who found inked on the hymnal's staffs

something solid and dependable, something she could follow
instinctively and with ease. Instead I sat and squinted

at the infinitely erasable ledger of a slate roof's ridge, its un-margined
            edges,
its sloped-away planes, its steeple and spires, its chaos of pigeons,

and tried to narrate something other than gray, gray, gray, gray.
And now when I picture the scene, I see late fall, drizzle,

the windshield hemmed and veined with rain, though in the car
I'm not the least bit cold—and that's what I tell my mother I remember,

that when she looked out a window beside me, I was never cold.

Running on a Chilly Morning

Some days it feels as if the wind is what pares
my flesh closer and closer to bone, what scrapes
skin from the tips of my cheeks and the place
on my hips where a child would ride, if it had
anything to grip—as if I could pose on a hill
and be chiseled.
                    I know that's not how it works.

I know that even birds can grow plump,
despite the constant scouring of wind: ahead,
three black vultures waddle by the road,
and I breathe carrion and watch them fumble,
dazed and bloated from their gorge. Jealousy sears

like lactic acid in my gut. They are fat and bald
and beautiful, even swaddled in the stench
of rot. Even with their own shit drying on their legs.
And what kind of fool does that make me,
to wake and run myself tattered each morning,
when I'm neither predator nor prey?

I'd like to leap astride their putrid
wings and fly—I'd like to be feather-armed
and reed-boned, to be lighter—much lighter—
prone to scatter in a gust of wind, my limbs
unstrung, my blood untubed, finer
than a side stitch—no heavier than breath.

Groundskeeper

I'm certain they were placed with purpose,
these stacked tree limbs, their log-ends
flush so that their twigs surge and tangle

like a squalling sea. Maybe the groundskeeper did it.
Maybe he's a branch sculptor forging

a wooden statue of water that captures
its smirks and scowls, its fraying ridges,
its dimples and wrung froth.

He is taciturn, ruddy, drinks Bud, drives a pickup.
Keeps under his sink a jar of soap that leaches

motor oil from the skin; at diners, he orders
without looking at the menu. He does not ponder
his urge to sculpt, only defers to it as he does

his urges to eat, sleep, to trace his wife's collarbone
when she lies on her back. He clocks in early

and takes long lunches to work the twigs,
though his fingers peel like bark
from handling them—but he can't gauge

their balance in gloves, he says when his wife
sharpens her breath at his touch. *You work too hard,*

she tells him, kneading lotion into his skin,
and he nods
                        off and dreams her freckles spilling
into a pile on the sheets, her voice growing reedy

as a gull's. In his dream, the ocean's surface is a loom,
leaves have sprouted where his fingernails were,

he's diving over and under the water's warp,
weaving the waves' faces so they can see
to fling themselves endlessly against the sand.

Scatterling's Lament

Airport-bound at dawn, our stomachs tight-laced
from rising so early, we can all but hear the rusted
chain-link minutes grate past, all but see them flay
the shadows from the fog-webbed corn.
                                              On the radio,
an interview with a man widowed last year when
a suicidal Texas cop shot up a grocery store—
he speaks of his feet striking the floor mornings,
of the pen he grips to ink out spent hours

in his daybook. He breathes slowly, as if the air
were spiked with glass dust, then says, his voice
like tissue paper creasing, that if there's enough blue
overhead to make a pair of pants, he knows he'll be
okay. I crane past the steering wheel to check the sky—
But whose pants, I ask—it seems important.
John calls me back, points to a possum sprawled

on the asphalt, I swerve, and by the time my pulse
calms, someone from Washington is reading the hour's
headlines—protests, riots, stolen elections. And what
of the gunman? Had he lived, would he be soothed

knowing he haunts someone's thoughts, that for one
man, minutes can no longer glide past un-scragged
by his ghost? The host mentioned, as I jerked the car
back into my lane, that a charity donated crosses
for the victims but shipped too many and, by some
mistake or committee vote or gust of pure-blue clemency,
the extra was placed over the gunman's grave.
On the plaque, only his name and dates.

Dent de Lion (or Surviving a Long-Distance Relationship)

Who names a flower for a lion's tooth anyway?
It ought to reek of rotten meat or scrape the skin
from bare ankles—but then, I'm biased: my teeth
grind at night until bone powder crusts
my tongue and the bald roots throb.
                                          You tell me
I'm crazy, but the right kind of crazy, and I tell
you to meet me at the bus stop because I'm a-comin,
my love, and I'll be held together somehow—
scotch-taped, dipped in plaster, baked in a cheese
soufflé—we've got dinner plans and I'll be
god-damned if I can't hold my own spoon.

Chronic Religion

Stop taking planes everywhere, already!
Every time you call, you're in a different city—
Missoula, Charleston, Schenectady, Tulsa—it's
unsettling, like stretching the crick in my neck

and noticing crystals affixed to the ten-foot
ceiling of a concrete stairwell, or realizing
I'm reciting the Lord's prayer while I scan
the news for crashes. You want flying?

I had a dream last week about a wooden
chestplate slatted like shutters, with wings
hinged behind. I grabbed your hand
and flapped those wings and lifted us home

from the bowling alley, our toes brushing
shit-splattered rooftops. Except I sweated so hard
it soaked through the wood and I woke with sore
shoulders. What is it about faith that makes it act

like canned food? So easy to scoff at when times
are good, so appealing during a crisis. Now
the economy's kaput and we're all getting
fatter—I say print bible verses on corn chips,

decelerate the binge. Better yet, quit wiping
the chalice at communion and start an epidemic
of canker sores, so whole congregations
are tonguing the tender insides of their cheeks

all week, simultaneously stung and thrilled
by the whitehot flash of pain—

that'll keep Jesus on their minds. But the Gideons
opt for a more traditional method,

press tiny testaments into my hands, drop them
in my purse when I pass, like I need
the extra weight in there, like I've got millions
to blow on chiropractic bills.

Grief as a Half-Swallowed Kite

Running one morning, I see a dead goldfinch
near the curb, a second bird hopping at its feet—
tiny, electric yellow, it beaks out a reedy cry

(whether in ritual or distress I can't tell) and waits
too long to fly away from me, as if unsure for a moment
whether to leave at all, as if moored to its mate

by its too-heavy grief. I've seen this before.
At my pépère's wake, my mémère greeted everyone calmly,
the picture of acceptance after her husband's

gradual atrophy, offering sandwiches and touching
our cheeks, so that the bright-lit room all but lurched
when my uncle led her to the casket and she buckled,

shoulders wrenching, and reached for the folded hands.
And this is what I've filed in my mind under *grief*,
Mémère wilted toward her paraffin husband,

the scene stark in unscreened light, as if grief were too gauche
to avert its kilowatt glare, even as it ransacked her limbs,
even as its name, *grief*, sparked our tongues and disappeared.

But grief is like that: in the body, convulsing;
in the mouth, a treble-clef trill. That's what makes it bearable:
its grace, its buoyancy, its kite-force unreeling from our tongues

even as it anchors itself inside us, even as we half-choke
on its tail. It's why we welcome near-strangers at wakes:
that their grief, being lighter than our own, might lift us.

ACKNOWLEDGEMENTS

Many thanks to the editors of the following publications,
where some of these poems first appeared.

Bellevue Literary Review, "Someone Else's Pain" and "I Sit in Mrs.
Eder's Sunday School Class"; *City of the Big Shoulders: Poems about
Chicago*, "Arbor Dementia" (as "Emerald Ash"); *cream city review*,
"The Gospel of Household Plants"; *Fourth River*, "My Father's
Moonlilies"; *Greensboro Review*, "Grief as a Half-Swallowed Kite";
Harpur Palate, "Departures"; *Hollins Critic*, "Migration"; *LUMINA*,
"On Bridge Street"; *New Delta Review*, "Accident"; *North American
Review*, "Dysphasia"; *Ploughshares*, "Precision"; *Post Road*, "Earl
Grey" and "Older Sister"; *Prairie Schooner*, "Three-Fingered Willy"
and "Mislaid Memory about Pigeons"; *RHINO*, "Ear Training"; *Salt
Hill*, "Limen"; *Threepenny Review*, "Two Purple Sponges"

"Thumb-Sucking" won an Academy of American Poets Prize in 2010,
and "We Were Waiting," "Mrs. Eder's Sunday School Class," and
"Someone Else's Pain" won a Dorothy Sargent Rosenberg Prize in
2011.

My thanks, also, to everyone who helped make this book possible
through tireless support, encouragement, reading, and advising:
Allison Joseph, Judy Jordan, and Rodney Jones; the MFA students
and Irish Studies program at Southern Illinois University; my
parents; and Danielle, Kristin, Marissa, Lucia, and, yes, even John.

ABOUT THE AUTHOR

Brenna Lemieux has been lucky enough to live and write in Maryland, Pennsylvania, Illinois, Paris, and Galway. She has a BA in English and French from Bucknell University and an MFA in poetry from Southern Illinois University Carbondale. She currently lives in Chicago, where she works, writes, runs, and performs improvised comedy.

QUERCUS
Review
P R E S S

QUERCUS
Review
P R E S S

QUERCUS
Review
P R E S S

QUERCUS
Review
P R E S S

www.ingramcontent.com/pod-product-compliance
Lightning Source LLC
Chambersburg PA
CBHW051843040426
42447CB00006B/680

* 9 780692 529102 *